THE
BENJAMIN FRANKLIN BOOK OF QUOTES

A COLLECTION OF SPEECHES,
QUOTATIONS, ESSAYS AND
ADVICE FROM AMERICA'S MOST
PROLIFIC FOUNDING FATHER

EDITED BY TRAVIS HELLSTROM

hatherleigh

Hatherleigh Press is committed to preserving and protecting the natural resources of the earth. Environmentally responsible and sustainable practices are embraced within the company's mission statement.

Visit us at www.hatherleighpress.com and register online for free offers, discounts, special events, and more.

The Benjamin Franklin Book of Quotes

Text Copyright © 2024 Travis Hellstrom

Library of Congress Cataloging-in-Publication Data is available.

ISBN: 978-1-57826-980-8

COVER DESIGN BY CAROLYN KASPER

Printed in the United States

10 9 8 7 6 5 4 3 2 1

CONTENTS

INTRODUCTION

F RANKLIN WAS a true renaissance
man. He was a candlemaker, printer,
editor, columnist, writer, author, entre-
preneur, scientist, philanthropist, community
organizer, statesman, humorist, humanitarian
and in his free time, the discoverer of the Gulf
stream and creator of Daylight Savings Time.

It amazes me when I think about all he
accomplished during his lifetime. I love revis-
iting his life through his wonderful quotes;
I even have his picture up on my office wall.
He inspires me to do more with the time I
have been given while also maintaining a
sense of humor about all of it at the same time.

Here in *The Benjamin Franklin Book of
Quotes*, we have brought together some of his

greatest thoughts. It's a beautiful collection for big fans and the new admirers of this great man.

Franklin was born at a time when witches were rumored to be real and he died at the dawn of the modern age. It is an age that, to a surprising degree, he himself helped shape. He came from a society where class determined one's station in life and he helped create a country where merit and ability could flourish. In a rigid world of orthodoxy and dogma, he believed to the core of his soul in the virtues of tolerance and compromise. The quintessential optimist, he never doubted, even for a moment, that the future of humanity lay in the infinite power of human reason.

Benjamin Franklin & Virtue

"Be in general virtuous,
and you will be happy."

B EFORE DIVING into Ben Franklin's
greatest quotes, it's important to
recognize the importance of Virtue
in Franklin's life. In *The Autobiography of
Benjamin Franklin*, we find a list of thirteen
virtues that "occurr'd to me as necessary or
desirable." Throughout his life, Franklin kept
a small notebook where he kept track of these
virtues and how he was developing them into
consistent habits.

These names of virtues, with their precepts, were:

Temperance. Eat not to dullness; drink not to elevation.

Silence. Speak not but what may benefit others or yourself; avoid trifling conversation.

Order. Let all your things have their places; let each part of your business have its time.

Resolution. Resolve to perform what you ought; perform without fail what you resolve.

Frugality. Make no expense but to do good to others or yourself, i.e., waste nothing.

Industry. Lose no time; be always employ'd in something useful; cut off all unnecessary actions.

Sincerity. Use no hurtful deceit; think innocently and justly, and, if you speak, speak accordingly.

Justice. Wrong none by doing injuries or omitting the benefits that are your duty.

Moderation. Avoid extremes; forbear resenting injuries so much as you think they deserve.

Cleanliness. Tolerate no uncleanliness in body, clothes, or habitation.

Tranquility. Be not disturbed at trifles, or at accidents common or unavoidable.

Chastity. Rarely use venery but for health or offspring, never to dullness, weakness, or the injury of your own or another's peace or reputation.

Humility. Imitate Jesus and Socrates.

As for how to acquire these virtues, Franklin advised:

"My intention being to acquire the habitude of all these virtues, I judg'd it would be well not to distract my attention by attempting the whole at once, but to fix it on one of them at a time; and, when I should be master of that, then to proceed to another, and so on, till I should have gone thro' the thirteen; and, as the previous acquisition of some might facilitate the acquisition of certain others, I arrang'd them with that view, as they stand above. Temperance first, as it tends to procure that coolness and clearness of head, which is so necessary where constant vigilance was to be kept up, and guard maintained against the unremitting attraction of ancient habits, and the force of perpetual temptations.

This being acquir'd and establish'd, Silence would be more easy; and my desire being to gain knowledge at the same time that I improv'd in virtue, and considering that in conversation it was obtain'd rather by the use of the ears than of the tongue, and therefore wishing to break a habit I was getting into of prattling, punning, and joking, which only made me acceptable to trifling company, I gave Silence the second place."

"On the whole, tho' I never arrived at the Perfection I had been so ambitious of obtaining, but fell short of it," he wrote. *"Yet as I was, by the Endeavor, a better and a happier Man than I otherwise should have been if I had not attempted it."*

Of the many inventions (bifocals, odometer), accomplishments (US postal system,

Constitution) and experiments (the famous kite in a lightning storm) credited to Benjamin Franklin, none of his contributions to humanity outshine his brilliantly simple method for self-improvement.

"A bold and arduous project of arriving at moral perfection" is how America's least controversial and most industrious statesman described his method of personal betterment in his autobiography. He devised it so anyone could become their best possible self.

Franklin started by taking a critical look at his behavior, and he found that too often he traveled down unvirtuous roads that "natural inclination, custom or company might lead me into," as he put it. He concluded that he fell short of his ideal in more than a dozen areas of his life.

He ate and drank too much. He talked too much, especially about himself. He spent more money than he should. He didn't finish all his goals, and so on. In other words, he wrestled with the very same human urges, flaws and proclivities that we struggle with today.

Recognizing that, Franklin then focused on various virtues that, if mastered, would counteract his unwanted behavior. His list includes these thirteen: Temperance, Silence, Order, Resolution, Frugality, Industry, Sincerity, Justice, Moderation, Cleanliness, Tranquility, Chastity and Humility.

He chose thirteen because that number fits neatly into a calendar. Multiply it by four, and you get 52—the number of weeks in a year.

Franklin would take a single virtue at a time, work on it for a week and then move on to the next. Trying to fix everything that's wrong with you all at once is overwhelming, he decided. The virtuous path needs to be broken down to give each area some concentrated time of intention and effort. Every thirteen weeks, the cycle repeats itself.

He accounted for his progress on a chart and shared his plan and progress with friends. In his autobiography, Franklin recommends that all his readers take this thirteen virtues challenge if they seek moral perfection. He defines each virtue, explaining how they build upon one another and outlines how to chart one's progress.

Choose virtues that are meaningful to you. Consider asking your trusted friends about your faults, which can be blind spots for you. Franklin himself explained how Humility was added to his list after a friend told him he needed to work on it. "To be aware of a single shortcoming within oneself is more useful than to be aware of a thousand in someone else," His Holiness the Dalai Lama has since pointed out.

The themes in this book are inspired by the thirteen virtues that were so foundational for Franklin himself. I've updated them here to reflect the centuries that have passed and the wide variety of topics on which Franklin spoke and wrote.

Here are the themes in this book and the virtues that inspire them:

Themes	Franklin Virtue
Character	Temperance, Order
Education	Silence, Frugality
Happiness	Tranquility
Hard Work	Industry, Resolution
Humor	Moderation
Liberty	Justice
Wisdom	Sincerity, Cleanliness
Family	Chastity
Spirituality	Humility

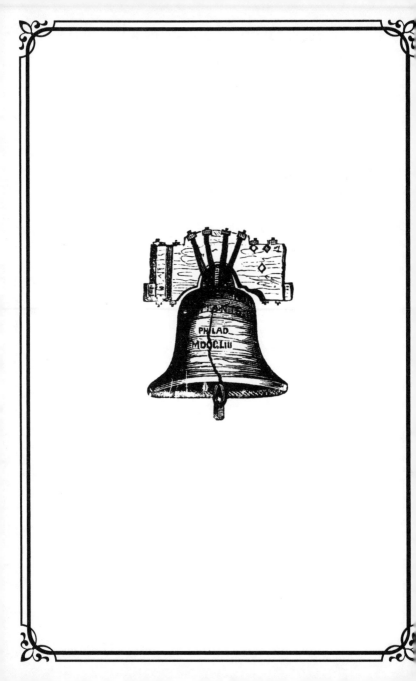

CHARACTER

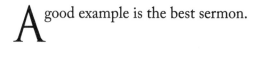

A good example is the best sermon.

A good conscience is a continual Christmas.

A perfect character might be attended with the inconvenience of being envied and hated; and that a benevolent man should allow a few faults in himself, to keep his friends in countenance.

A right heart exceeds all.

All the property that is necessary to a man for the conservation of the individual… is his natural right which none can justly deprive him of.

An equal dispensation of protection, rights, privileges, and advantages, is what every part is entitled to, and ought to enjoy.

Be at war with your vices, at peace with your neighbors, and let every new year find you a better man.

Glass, china, and reputation, are easily crack'd, and never well mended.

It is his honesty that brought upon him the character of a heretic.

History will also afford frequent opportunities of showing the necessity of a public religion, from its usefulness to the public; the advantage of a religious character among private persons; the mischiefs of superstition, and the excellency of the Christian religion above all others, ancient or modern.

Nothing is more important for the public wealth than to form and train youth in wisdom and virtue. Only a virtuous people are capable of freedom.

It takes many good deeds to build a good reputation, and only one bad one to lose it.

Only a virtuous people are capable of freedom. As nations become more corrupt and vicious, they have more need of masters.

We may give advice, but we cannot give conduct.

The best thing to give to your enemy is forgiveness; to an opponent, tolerance; to a friend, your heart; to your child, a good example; to a father, deference; to your mother, conduct that will make her proud of you; to yourself, respect; to all others, charity.

The proof of gold is fire.

There is much difference between imitating a good man and counterfeiting him.

There never was a good knife made of bad steel.

To be thrown upon one's own resources is to be cast into the very lap of fortune; for our faculties then undergo a development and display an energy of which they were previously unsusceptible.

Tricks and treachery are the practice of fools, that don't have brains enough, to be honest.

Whoever feels pain in hearing a good character of his neighbor, will feel a pleasure in the reverse. And those who despair to rise in distinction by their virtues, are happy if others can be depressed to a level of themselves.

What you seem to be, be really.

Who is strong? He that can conquer his bad habits.

What more valuable than Gold? Diamonds.
Than Diamonds? Virtue.

Wish not so much to live long as to live well.

On the whole, tho' I never arrived at the
Perfection I had been so ambitious of obtaining, but fell short of it. Yet as I was, by the
Endeavor, a better and a happier Man than I
otherwise should have been if I had not attempted it.

Hide not your Talents, they for Use were made. What's a Sun-Dial in the shade!

If you would not be forgotten as soon as you are dead, either write something worth reading or do something worth writing.

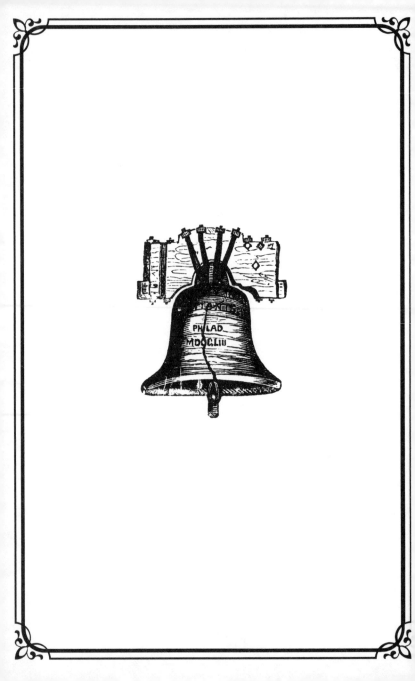

EDUCATION

An investment in knowledge pays the best dividends.

Average minds think and talk about things and actions.

Believe none of what you hear and half of what you see.

Change is the only constant in life. One's ability to adapt to those changes will determine your success in life.

Common sense is something that everyone needs, few have, and none think they lack.

Common sense without education is better than education without common sense.

Experience is the best teacher, but a fool will learn from no other.

Genius is the ability to hold one's vision steady until it becomes reality.

Genius without education is like silver in the mine.

God heals, and the doctor takes the fees.

Great minds think and talk about ideas.

He who would trade liberty for some temporary security deserves neither liberty nor security.

How do you become better tomorrow? By improving yourself, the world is made better. Be not afraid of growing too slowly. Be afraid of standing still. Forget your mistakes, but remember what they taught you. So how do you become better tomorrow? By becoming better today.

I am for doing good to the poor, but I differ in opinion about the means. I think the best way of doing good to the poor is not making them easy in poverty, but leading or driving them out of it.

If a man empties his purse into his head, no one can take it from him. An investment in knowledge always pays the best interest.

If everyone is thinking alike, then no one is thinking.

If you do tomorrow what you did today, you will get tomorrow what you got today.

Instead of cursing the darkness, light a candle.

It is the first responsibility of every citizen to question authority.

Little minds think and talk about people.

Make yourself sheep and the wolves will eat you.

Take the money in your wallet and invest it in your mind. And in return, your mind will fill up your wallet!

Tell me and I forget, teach me and I remember, involve me and I learn.

The only thing more expensive than education is ignorance.

To find out a girl's faults, praise her to her girlfriends.

We are all born ignorant, but one must work hard to remain stupid.

When you get into a tight place and everything goes against you, till it seems as though
you could not hold on a minute longer, never
give up then, for that is just the place and time
that the tide will turn.

When you're finished changing, you're
finished.

Where liberty dwells, there is my country.

Whoever would overthrow the liberty of a nation must begin by subduing the freedom of speech, a thing terrible to traitors.

Without freedom of thought, there can be no such thing as wisdom; and no such thing as public liberty without freedom of speech; which is the right of every man as far as by it he does not hurt or control the right of another; and this is the only check it ought to suffer and the only bounds it ought to know.

HAPPINESS

Happiness is not achieved by the conscious pursuit of happiness; it is generally the by-product of other activities.

A cheerful face is nearly as good for an invalid as healthy weather.

Be in general virtuous, and you will be happy.

By heaven we understand a state of happiness infinite in degree, and endless in duration.

Contentment makes poor men rich; discontent makes rich men poor.

Human felicity is produced not so much by great pieces of good fortune that seldom happen, as by little advantages that occur every day.

Keep in the sunlight. Happiness depends more on the inward disposition of mind than on outward circumstances.

Happiness is not achieved by the conscious pursuit of happiness; it is generally the by-product of other activities.

Do not anticipate trouble, or worry about what may never happen.

I was surprised to find myself so much fuller of Faults than I had imagined, but I had the Satisfaction of seeing them diminish.

If you teach a poor young man to shave himself, and keep his razor in order, you may contribute more to the happiness of his life than in giving him a thousand guineas.

If you would not be laughed at, be the first to laugh at yourself.

If you wouldn't live long, live well; for folly and wickedness shorten life.

In order to be happy you need a good dog, a good woman, and ready money.

It is much easier to suppress a first desire than to satisfy those that follow.

Money never made a man happy yet, nor will it. The more a man has, the more he wants. Instead of filling a vacuum, it makes one.

Dost thou love life? Then do not squander time; for that's the stuff life is made of.

The Constitution only guarantees the American people the right to pursue happiness. You have to catch it yourself.

Most men die from the neck up at age twenty-five because they stop dreaming.

On the whole, though I never arrived at the perfection I had been so ambitious of obtaining, but fell far short of it, yet I was, by the endeavor, a better and a happier man than I otherwise should have been had I not attempted it.

A true friend is the best possession.

The grand essentials of happiness are: something to do, something to love, and something to hope for.

~

The happiness of your life depends upon the quality of your thoughts.

~

There are two ways of being happy: We must either diminish our wants or augment our means—either may do—the result is the same and it is for each man to decide for himself and to do that which happens to be easier.

There are two ways to be happy: improve your reality or lower your expectations.

~

We are not so sensible of the greatest Health as of the least Sickness.

~

What is without us has no connection with happiness, only so far as the preservation of our lives and health depends upon it....Happiness springs immediately from the mind.

The best of all medicines is resting and fasting.

Happiness consists more in small conveniences or pleasures that occur every day, than in great pieces of good fortune that happen but seldom to a man in the course of his life.

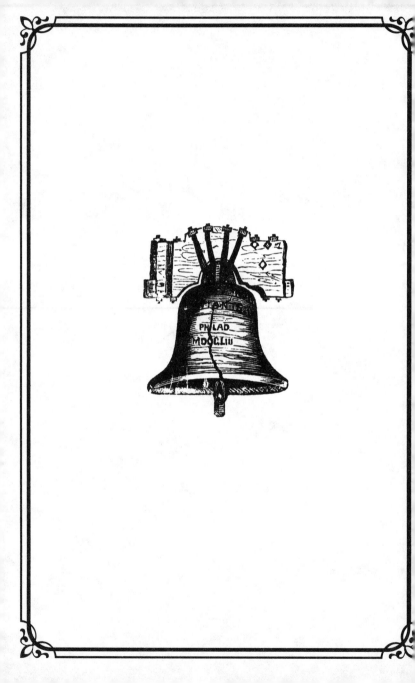

HARD WORK

Early to bed and early to rise makes a man healthy, wealthy, and wise.

An ounce of prevention is worth a pound of cure.

By failing to prepare, you are preparing to fail.

Diligence is the mother of good luck.

Employ thy time well, if thou meanest to gain leisure.

God helps those who help themselves.

Haste makes waste.

If you love life, don't waste time, for time is what life is made up of.

Lost time is never found again.

Motivation is when your teams put on work clothes.

No gains without pains.

Success is the residue of planning.

The problem with doing nothing is not knowing when you're finished.

To succeed, jump as quickly at opportunities as you do at conclusions.

Doing your best means never stop trying.

I never knew a man who was good at making excuses who was good at anything else.

Repeal that [welfare] law, and you will soon see a change in their manners....Six days shalt thou labor, though one of the old commandments long treated as out of date, will again be looked upon as a respectable precept; industry will increase, and with it plenty among the lower people; their circumstances will mend, and more will be done for their happiness by inuring them to provide for themselves than could be done by dividing all your estates among them.

In my youth, I traveled much, and I observed in different countries, that the more public provisions were made for the poor, the less they provided for themselves, and of course became poorer. And, on the contrary, the less was done for them, the more they did for themselves, and became richer.

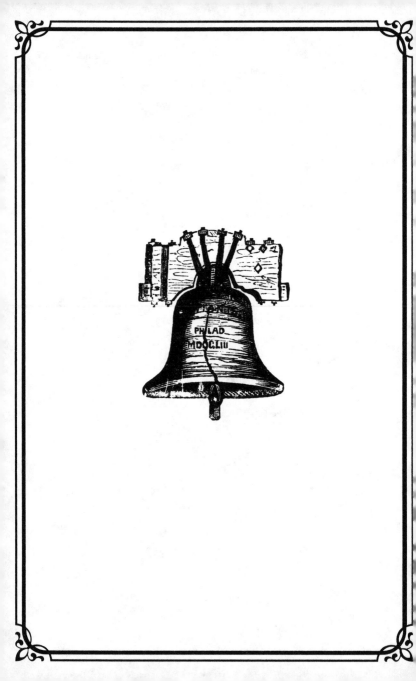

HUMOR

Better slip with foot than tongue.

The worst wheel of the cart makes the most noise.

He that is good for making excuses is seldom good for anything else.

In this world nothing can be said to be certain, except death and taxes.

Fish and visitors stink in three days.

Behold the rain which descends from heaven upon our vineyards; there it enters the roots of the vines, to be changed into wine; a constant proof that God loves us, and loves to see us happy.

Wine is constant proof that God loves us and loves to see us happy.

He that lies down with dogs, shall rise up with fleas.

Three may keep a secret, if two of them are dead.

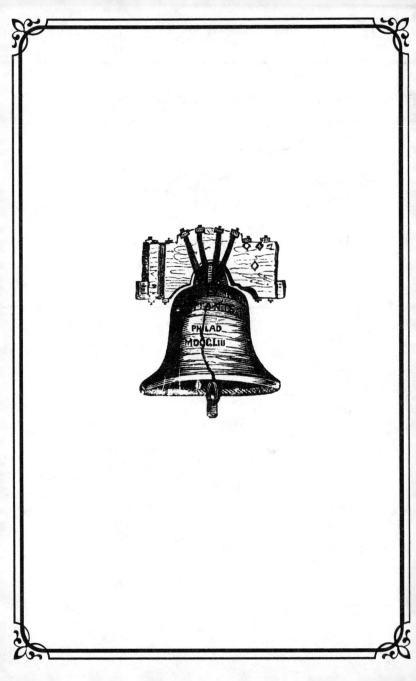

LIBERTY

God grant that not only the love of liberty but a thorough knowledge of the rights of man may pervade all the nations of the earth, so that a philosopher may set his foot anywhere on its surface and say: This is my country.

⟳

Every man…is, of common right, and by the laws of God, a freeman, and entitled to the free enjoyment of liberty.

Freedom of speech is a principal pillar of a free government; when this support is taken away, the constitution of a free society is dissolved, and tyranny is erected on its ruins. Republics...derive their strength and vigor from a popular examination into the action of the magistrates.

Justice will not be served until those who are unaffected are as outraged as those who are.

From a persuasion that equal liberty was originally the portion, it is still the birthright of all men.

Frequent recurrence to fundamental principles...[is] absolutely necessary to preserve the blessings of liberty and keep a government free.

Ordaining of laws in favor of one part of the nation to the prejudice and oppression of another is certainly the most erroneous and mistaken policy...An equal dispensation of protection, rights, privileges, and advantages, is what every part is entitled to, and ought to enjoy.

Rebellion to tyrants is obedience to God.
—*Proposed by Franklin for the motto of the Great Seal of the United States*

Our new Constitution is now established, and has an appearance that promises permanency; but in this world nothing can be said to be certain, except death and taxes!

Our cause is the cause of all mankind…we are fighting for their liberty in defending our own.

Security without liberty is called prison.

This [the U.S. Constitution] is likely to be administered for a course of years and then end in despotism…when the people shall become so corrupted as to need despotic government, being incapable of any other.

⁓

The more the people are discontented with the oppression of taxes, the greater the need the prince has of money to distribute among his partisans and pay the troops that are to suppress all resistance and enable him to plunder at pleasure.

Sell not…liberty to purchase power.

Those who beat their swords into plowshares usually end up plowing for those who kept their swords.

Those who desire to give up freedom in order to gain security will not have, nor do they deserve, either one.

Without freedom of thought there can be no such thing as wisdom; and no such thing as public liberty, without freedom of speech.

He that falls in love with himself will have no rivals.

There never was a good war or a bad peace.

The noblest question in the world is: 'What good may I do in it?'

~

War is when the government tells you who the bad guy is. Revolution is when you decide that for yourself.

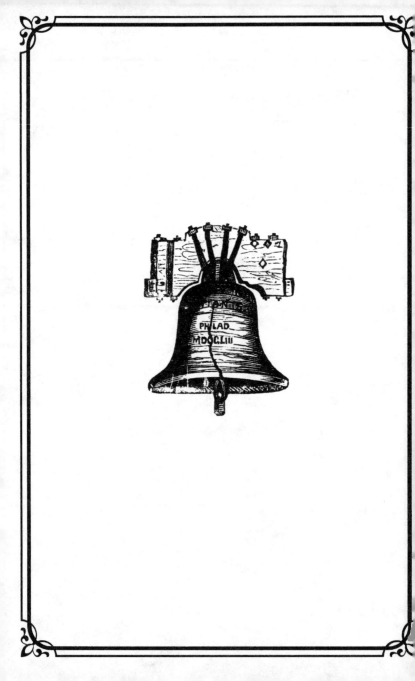

WISDOM

The doorstep to the temple of wisdom is a knowledge of our own ignorance.

He that can have patience can have what he will.

A penny saved is a penny earned.

And now I speak of thanking God, I desire with all humility to acknowledge that I owe the mentioned happiness of my past life to His kind providence, which lead me to the means I used and gave them success.

Blame-all and Praise-all are two blockheads.

Be civil to all; sociable to many; familiar with few; friend to one; enemy to none.

Beware of little expenses. A small leak will sink a great ship.

At the working man's house hunger looks in but dares not enter.

A house is not a home unless it contains food and fire for the mind as well as the body.

He that would live in peace and at ease, must not speak all he knows or judge all he sees.

Have you something to do tomorrow? Do it today.

He that lives upon hope will die fasting.

Having emerged from the poverty and obscurity in which I was born and bred, to a state of affluence and some degree of reputation in the world, and having gone so far through life with a considerable share of felicity, the conducing means I made use of, which with the blessing of God so well succeeded, my posterity may like to know, as they may find some of them suitable to their own situations, and therefore fit to be imitated.

Speak little, do much.

He who has never failed somewhere, that man cannot be great.

Honesty is the best policy.

It's easy to see, hard to foresee.

Look before, or you'll find yourself behind.

Love your enemies, for they tell you your faults.

Many people die at twenty-five and aren't buried until they are seventy-five.

Never leave that till tomorrow which you can do today.

Never ruin an apology with an excuse.

Pardoning the bad, is injuring the good.

~

Who is wise? He that learns from everyone. Who is powerful? He that governs his passions. Who is rich? He that is content. Who is that? Nobody.

~

The doors of wisdom are never shut.

Search others for their virtues, thy self for thy vices.

There are three things extremely hard: steel, a diamond, and to know oneself.

We must all hang together, or assuredly, we shall all hang separately.

Well done is better than well said.

Whatever is begun in anger ends in shame.

Don't throw stones at your neighbors if your own windows are glass.

When in doubt, don't.

You may delay, but time will not.

I hope…that all mankind will at length…have reason and sense enough to settle their differences without cutting throats.

Without continual growth and progress, such words as improvement, achievement, and success have no meaning.

It is better to take many injuries than to give one.

When you're good to others, you're best to yourself.

Remember not only to say the right thing in the right place but far more difficult still, to leave unsaid the wrong thing at the tempting moment.

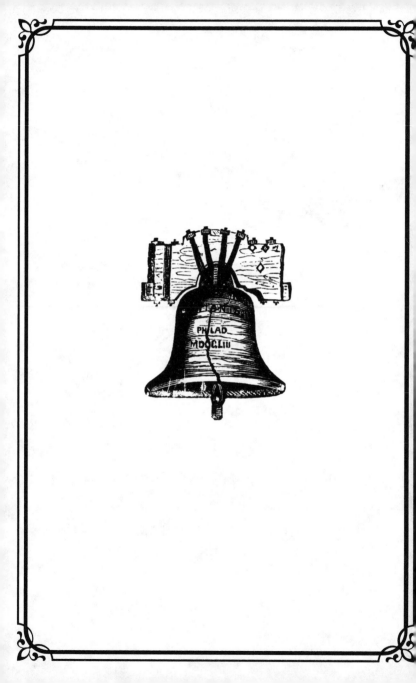

FAMILY

My family is my life, and everything else comes second as far as what's important to me.

The memories we make with our family are everything.

Everyone needs a house to live in, but a supportive family is what builds a home.

Family and friends are hidden treasures, seek them out and enjoy their riches.

He that raises a large family does, indeed, while he lives to observe them, stand a broader mark for sorrow; but then he stands a broader mark for pleasure too.

Keep your eyes wide open before marriage, half shut afterwards.

Families ought to be noisy.

Women are books, and men the readers be.

And as to the Cares, they are chiefly what attend the bringing up of Children; and I would ask any Man who has experienced it, if they are not the most delightful Cares in the World; and if from that Particular alone, he does not find the Bliss of a double State much greater, instead of being less than he expected.

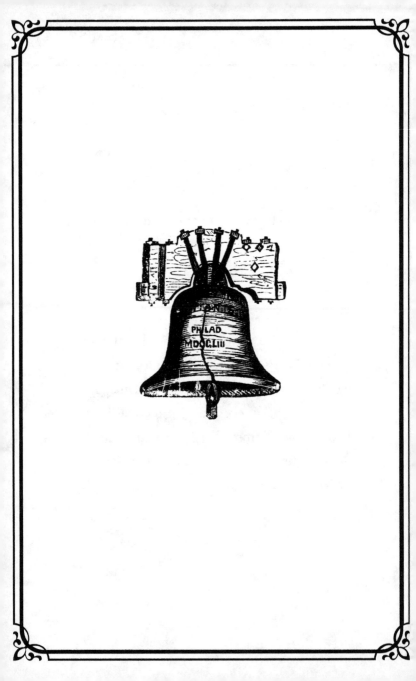

SPIRITUALITY

When you're down to nothing, God is up to something. The faithful see the invisible, believe the incredible, and then receive the impossible.

~

Whoever shall introduce into public affairs the principles of primitive Christianity will change the face of the world.

How many observe Christ's birthday! How few, His precepts!

I believe in one God, creator of the Universe. That he governs it by his Providence. That he ought to be worshipped. That the most acceptable Service we render to him is doing good to his other Children…Vital religion has always suffered when orthodoxy is more regarded than virtue.

If we look back in history for the character of the present sects in Christianity, we shall find a few that have not in their turns been persecutors and complainers of persecution. The primitive Christians thought persecution extremely wrong in the Pagans, but practiced it one another. The first Protestants of the Church of England blamed persecution in the Romish Church, but practiced it upon the Puritans. They found it wrong in Bishops, but fell into the practice themselves both there (England) and New England.

I have lived, Sir, a long time and the longer I live, the more convincing proofs I see of this truth—that God governs in the affairs of men. And if a sparrow cannot fall to the ground without His notice, is it probable that an empire can rise without his aid? We have been assured, Sir, in the sacred writings that "except the Lord build they labor in vain that build it." I firmly believe this, and I also believe that without his concurring aid we shall succeed in this political building no better than the Builders of Babel.

Lighthouses are more helpful than churches.

The way to see by Faith is to shut the Eye of
Reason.

When a religion is good, I conceive it will
support itself; and when it does not support
itself, and God does not take care to support
it so that its professors are obliged to call for
help of the civil power, 'tis a sign, I apprehend,
of its being a bad one.

Death takes no bribes.

The rapid progress of the sciences makes me, at times, sorry that I was born so soon. Imagine the power that man will have over matter a few hundred years from now. We may learn how to remove gravity from large masses and float them over great distances, agriculture will double its produce with less labor, all diseases will surely be cured, even old age. If only the moral sciences could be improved as well. Perhaps men would cease to be wolves to one another and human beings could learn to be...human.

SELECTED
WRITINGS &
SPEECHES

SPEECH AT THE CONSTITUTIONAL CONVENTION

September 17, 1787

I confess that there are several parts of this constitution which I do not at present approve, but I am not sure I shall never approve them. For having lived long, I have experienced many instances of being obliged by better information, or fuller consideration, to change opinions even on important subjects, which I once thought right, but found to be otherwise. It is therefore that the older I grow, the more apt I am to doubt my own judgment, and to pay more respect to the judgment of others. Most men, indeed as well as most sects in Religion, think themselves in possession of all truth, and that wherever others differ from them it is so far error. Steele, a Protestant, in a Dedication tells the Pope that the only difference between our Churches in their opinions of the certainty of their doctrines is the Church of Rome is infallible and the Church of England is never in the wrong. But though many private persons think almost as highly of their own infallibility as of that of their sect, few express it so naturally as a certain French lady, who in a dispute with her sister, said, "I don't know how it happens, Sister, but I meet with nobody but myself, that's always in the right; Il n'y a que moi qui a toujours raison." In these sentiments, Sir,

I agree to this Constitution with all its faults, if they are such; because I think a general Government necessary for us, and there is no form of Government but what may be a blessing to the people if well administered, and believe farther that this is likely to be well administered for a course of years, and can only end in Despotism, as other forms have done before it, when the people shall become so corrupted as to need despotic Government, being incapable of any other.

Although there is no definitive record of Benjamin Franklin delivering a speech at the Constitutional Convention in 1787, Franklin did make some remarks during the convention, particularly towards the end of the proceedings.

As the story goes, Franklin spoke in support of the Constitution despite its imperfections. While the exact wording of Franklin's remarks varies in different historical accounts, a popular version includes the above. It's worth noting that while these sentiments are often attributed to Franklin, the precise words may have been paraphrased or embellished over time. However, the message here conveyed aligns with Franklin's pragmatic and conciliatory approach to governance.

THE WAY TO WEALTH

1758

Courteous Reader,

I have heard that nothing gives an author so great pleasure as to find his works respectfully quoted by other learned authors. This pleasure I have seldom enjoyed; for though I have been, if I may say it without vanity, an eminent author of almanacks annually now a full quarter of a century, my brother authors in the same way, for what reason I know not, have ever been very sparing in their applauses; and no other author has taken the least notice of me; so that, did not my writings produce me some solid pudding, the great deficiency of praise would have quite discouraged me.

I concluded at length, that the people were the best judges of my merit; for they buy my works; and besides, in my rambles, where I am not personally known, I have frequently heard one or other of my adages repeated, with, as Poor Richard says, at the end on't. This gave me some satisfaction, as it showed not only that my instructions were regarded, but discovered likewise some respect for my authority; and I own, that to encourage the practice of remembering and repeating those wise sentences, I have sometimes quoted myself with great gravity.

Judge, then, how much I must have been gratified by an incident I am going to relate to you. I stopped my horse lately, where a great number of people were collected at an auction of merchants' goods. The hour of sale not being come, they were conversing on the badness of the times; and one of the company called to a plain, clean, old man, with white locks: "Pray, Father Abraham, what think you of the times? Will not these heavy taxes quite ruin the country? How shall we ever be able to pay them? What would you advise us to?" Father Abraham stood up and replied: "If you'd have my advice, I'll give it you in short; for, 'A word to the wise is enough,' as Poor Richard says." They joined in desiring him to speak his mind, and gathering round him, he proceeded as follows:

"Friends," said he, "the taxes are indeed very heavy, and if those laid on by the Government were the only ones we had to pay, we might more easily discharge them; but we have many others, and much more grievous to some of us. We are taxed twice as much by our idleness, three times as much by our pride, and four times as much by our folly; and from these taxes the commissioners cannot ease or deliver us by allowing an abatement. However, let us hearken to good advice, and something may be done for us; God helps them that help themselves, as Poor Richard says.

"**I.** It would be thought a hard Government that should tax its people one-tenth part of their time, to be employed in its service; but idleness taxes many of us much more; sloth, by bringing on diseases, absolutely shortens life. Sloth, like rust, consumes faster than labor wears; while the used key is always bright, as Poor Richard says. But dost thou love life, then do not squander time, for that's the stuff life is made of, as Poor Richard says. How much more than is necessary do we spend in sleep, forgetting that The sleeping fox catches no poultry, and that There will be sleeping enough in the grave, as Poor Richard says.

"II. If time be of all things the most precious, wasting time must be, as Poor Richard says, the greatest prodigality; since, as he elsewhere tells us, Lost time is never found again; and what we call time enough always proves little enough. Let us, then, up and be doing, and doing to the purpose; so by diligence shall we do more with less perplexity. Sloth makes all things difficult, but industry all easy; and He that riseth late must trot all day, and shall scarce overtake his business at night; while Laziness travels so slowly, that Poverty soon overtakes him. Drive thy business, let not that drive thee; and Early to bed, and early to rise, makes a man healthy, wealthy, and wise, as Poor Richard says.

"So what signifies wishing and hoping for better times? We may make these times better if we bestir ourselves. Industry need not wish, as Poor Richard says, and He that lives upon hope will die fasting. There are no gains without pains; then Help, hands, for I have no lands; or if I have, they are smartly taxed. And as Poor Richard likewise observes, He that hath a trade hath an estate, and He that hath a calling hath an office of profit and honor; but then the trade must be worked at, and the calling well followed, or neither the estate nor the office will enable us to pay our taxes. If we are industrious, we shall never starve; for, At the working man's house hunger looks in, but dares not enter. Nor will the bailiff or the constable enter, for Industry pays debts, while despair increaseth them, says Poor Richard. What though you have found no treasure, nor has any rich relation left you a legacy, Diligence is the mother of good luck, as Poor Richard says; and God gives all things to industry. Then plough deep, while sluggards sleep, and you shall have corn to sell and to keep, says Poor Dick. Work while it is called to-day, for you know not how much you may be hindered to-morrow. One to-day is worth two to-morrows, as Poor Richard says; and farther, Never leave that till to-morrow which you can do to-day. If you were a servant, would you not be ashamed that a good master should catch you idle? Are you then your own master? Be ashamed to catch yourself idle, as Poor Dick says. When there is so much to be done for yourself, your family, your country, and your gracious King, be up by peep of day! Let not the sun look down and say, Inglorious here so that, as Poor Richard says, A life of leisure and a life of laziness are two things. Do you imagine that sloth will afford you more comfort than labor? No, for as Poor Richard says, Trouble springs from idleness, and grievous toil from needless ease. Many, without labor, would live by their wits only, but they break for want of stock; whereas industry gives comfort, and plenty, and respect. Fly pleasures, and they'll follow you. The diligent spinner has a large shift; and Now I have a sheep and a cow, everybody bids me good morrow, all which is well said by Poor Richard.

"But with our industry we must likewise be steady, settled, and careful, and oversee our own affairs with our own eyes, and not trust too much to others; for, as Poor Richard says,

I never saw an oft-removed tree,
Nor yet an oft-removed family,
That throve so well as those that
settled be.

And again, Three removes are as bad as a fire; and again, Keep thy shop, and thy shop will keep thee; and again, If you would have your business done, go; if not, send.

"And again,

He that by the plough would thrive,
Himself must either hold or drive.

And again, The eye of a master will do more work than both his hands; and again, Want of care does us more damage than want of knowledge; and again, Not to oversee workmen, is to leave them your purse open.

Trusting too much to others' care is the ruin of many; for, as the Almanac says, In the affairs of this world, men are saved, not by faith, but by the want of it; but a man's own care is profitable; for, saith Poor Dick, Learning is to the studious, and Riches to the careful, as well as Power to the bold, and Heaven to the virtuous. And farther, If you would have a faithful servant, and one that you like, serve yourself. A little neglect may breed great mischief; for want of a nail the shoe was lost; for want of a shoe the horse was lost; and for want of a horse the rider was lost; being overtaken and slain by the enemy; all for want of a little care about a horse-shoe nail.

"So much for industry, my friends, and attention to one's own business; but to these we must add frugality, if we would make our industry more certainly successful. A man may, if he knows not how to save as he gets, keep his nose to the grindstone all his life, and die not worth a groat at last. A fat kitchen makes a lean will, as Poor Richard says; and

> Many estates are spent in the getting,
> Since women for tea forsook spinning
>   and knitting,
> And men for punch forsook hewing
>   and splitting.

"If you would be wealthy, says he in another almanack, think of saving as well as of getting. The Indies have not made Spain rich, because her outgoes are greater than her incomes.

"Away then with your expensive follies, and you will not have so much cause to complain

"Here you are all got together at this sale of fineries and knick-knacks. You call them goods; but if you do not take care, they will prove evils to some of you. You expect they will be sold cheap, and perhaps they may for less than they cost; but if you have no occasion for them, they must be dear to you. Remember what Poor Richard says, Buy what thou hast no need of, and ere long thou shalt sell thy necessaries. And again, At a great pennyworth pause a while. He means, that perhaps the cheapness is apparent only, and not real; or the bargain, by straitening thee in thy business, may do thee more harm than good. For in another place he says, Many have been ruined by buying good pennyworths. Again, Poor Richard says, 'Tis foolish to lay out money in a purchase of repentance; and yet this folly is practiced every day at auctions, for want of minding the Almanac. Many a one, for the sake of finery on the back, have gone with a hungry belly and half-starved their families. Silks and satins, scarlet and velvets, as Poor Richard says, put out the kitchen fire. These are not the necessaries of life; they can scarcely be called the conveniences, and yet only because they look pretty, how many want to have them. The artificial wants of mankind thus become more numerous than the natural; and, as Poor Dick says, For one poor person, there are a hundred indigent.

"By these, and other extravagancies, the genteel are reduced to poverty, and forced to borrow of those whom they formerly despised, but who, through industry and frugality, have maintained their standing; in which case it appears plainly, that A ploughman on his legs is higher than a gentleman on his knees, as Poor Richard says. Perhaps they have had a small estate left them, which they knew not the getting of; they think 'tis day, and will never be night; that a little to be spent out of so much is not worth minding; but Always taking out of the meal-tub, and never putting in, soon comes to the bottom, as Poor Richard says; and then, When the well is dry, they know the worth of water. But this they might have known before, if they had taken his advice; If you would know the value of money, go and try to borrow some; for, he that goes a borrowing goes a sorrowing, as Poor Richard says; and, indeed, so does he that lends to such people, when he goes to get it in again. Poor Dick farther advises, and says,

Fond pride of dress is sure a very curse;
Ere fancy you consult, consult
    your purse.

"And again, Pride is as loud a beggar as Want, and a great deal more saucy. When you have bought one fine thing, you must buy ten more, that your appearance may be all of a piece; but Poor Dick says, 'Tis easier to suppress the first desire than to satisfy all that follow it. And 'tis as truly folly for the poor to ape the rich, as for the frog to swell in order to equal the ox.

Great estates may venture more,
But little boats should keep near shore.

"'Tis, however, a folly soon punished; for, as Poor Richard says, Pride that dines on vanity, sups on contempt. Pride breakfasted with Plenty, dined with Poverty, and supped with Infamy.

"And, after all, of what use is this pride of appearance, for which so much is risked, so much is suffered? It cannot promote health, or ease pain; it makes no increase of merit in the person; it creates envy; it hastens smisfortune.

"But what madness must it be to run in debt for these superfluities? We are offered, by the terms of this sale, six months' credit; and that perhaps has induced some of us to attend it, because we cannot spare the ready money, and hope now to be fine without it. But, ah! think what you do when you run in debt; you give to another power over your liberty. If you cannot pay at the time, you will be ashamed to see your creditor; you will be in fear when you speak to him, you will make poor, pitiful, sneaking excuses, and by degrees come to lose your veracity, and sink into base downright by confining you in gaol for life, or by selling you for a servant, if you should not be able to pay him! When you have got your bargain, you may, perhaps, think little of payment; but Creditors, Poor Richard tells us, have better memories than debtors; and in another place says, Creditors are a superstitious sect, great observers of set days and times. The day comes round before you are aware, and the demand is made before you are prepared to satisfy it; or if you bear your debt in mind, the term which at first seemed so long, will, as it lessens, appear extremely short. Time will seem to have added wings to his heels as well as shoulders. Those have a short Lent, saith Poor Richard, who owe money to be paid at Easter. Then since, as he says, The borrower is a slave to the lender, and the debtor to the creditor, disdain the chain, preserve your freedom; and maintain your independency.

Be industrious and free; be frugal and free. At present, perhaps, you may think yourselves in thriving circumstances, and that you can bear a little extravagance without injury; but

> "For age and want, save while you may;
> No morning sun lasts a whole day,

as Poor Richard says. Gain may be temporary and uncertain; but ever, while you live, expense is constant and certain; and 'Tis easier to build two chimneys than to keep one in fuel, as Poor Richard says. So, Rather go to bed supperless than rise in debt.

"Get what you can, and what you get hold, 'Tis the stone that will turn all your lead into gold, as Poor Richard says. And when you have got the philosopher's stone, sure you will no longer complain of bad times, or the difficulty of paying taxes.

"This doctrine, my friends, is reason and wisdom; but after all, do not depend too much upon your own industry, and frugality, and prudence, though excellent things; for they may all be blasted without the blessing of Heaven; and therefore, ask that blessing humbly, and be not uncharitable to those that at present seem to want it, but comfort and help them. Remember Job suffered, and was afterward prosperous.

"And now, to conclude, Experience keeps a dear school, but fools will learn in no other, as Poor Richard says, and scarce in that; for it is true, We may give advice, but we cannot give conduct. However, remember this, They that won't be counseled, can't be helped, as Poor Richard says; and farther, That If you will not hear Reason, she'll surely rap your knuckles."

Thus the old gentleman ended his harangue. The people heard it, and approved the doctrine, and immediately practiced the contrary, just as if it had been a common sermon; for the auction opened, and they began to buy extravagantly.

I found the good man had thoroughly studied my Almanacks, and digested all I had dropped on those topics during the course of twenty-five years. The frequent mention he made of me must have tired anyone else, but my vanity was wonderfully delighted with it, though I was conscious that not a tenth part of the wisdom was my own, which he ascribed to me, but rather the gleanings that I had made of the sense of all ages and nations. However, I resolved to be the better for the echo of it;

and, though I had at first determined to buy stuff for a new coat, I went away resolved to wear my old one a little longer. Reader, if thou wilt do the same, thy profit will be as great as mine. I am, as ever, thine to serve thee,

—RICHARD SAUNDERS

"The Way to Wealth" is a famous essay written by Benjamin Franklin, originally published as a preface to the 1758 edition of his annual almanac, Poor Richard's Almanack. *Presented here in its entirety, the essay is filled with Franklin's timeless wisdom on the virtues of industry, frugality, and self-reliance, and it continues to be widely read and quoted to this day.*

On the Death
of His Brother,
John Franklin

To Madam Franklin,
My ever dear Sister,

I long since determined, to write to you on the subject of your afflictive loss in the death of our dear brother. Your own good understanding, and the advice of your friends, will better direct you how to bear it, than any thing that can be written. I shall therefore confine myself to such general observations only, as may occur in the course of the letter.

In this world nothing can be said to be certain, except death and taxes. The first, is the lot of all, and on many occasions a relief from the worst of evils. The second, like the drop of a honeycomb, hangs suspended, almost eternally, till by time, it is transformed into the mead of some fortunate heir.

Our brother is, as you say, no more. But in his case the change was not from bad to worse, but, as we have all reason to hope, and believe, from good to better. He had suffered much by long continued bodily indisposition, which had greatly diminished his strength, and affected his spirits. This often made his life burdensome to himself, though it was made as agreeable as possible to others by his cheerful, complaisant temper. He was an affectionate husband, a tender parent, and a kind, obliging, generous friend; and his removal must have left a gap in the hearts of all who knew him, especially in yours and his children's. But let not this increase your grief. Rather take comfort from the persuasion that you will meet him again, in a better and happier state of existence. Let your good example instruct your children in the means to be used for obtaining that happiness, and assure them, that if they are good, they shall certainly meet their papa again; where, sorrow shall be unknown, and the joys of a virtuous life shall be without end.

This is the most material, and most comfortable consideration in religion. For my own part, my mind has for some time been past wavering on that point. I believe in one God, Creator of the universe. That he governs it by his providence. That he ought to be worshipped. That the most acceptable service we can render to him is doing good to his other children. That the soul of man is immortal, and will be treated with justice in another life respecting its conduct in this. These I take to be fundamental points in all sound religion, and I regard them as you do, with a pure heart, a pious mind, and a grateful sense of the infinite obligations we have to that great and benevolent Being who has made us, and whose goodness we experience every moment.

I have given you my thoughts on the principal subject of your letter. I now proceed to acquaint you with the particulars of our family affairs, and shall conclude with my hearty wishes for your health and happiness, and that of your children.

"On the Death of His Brother, John Franklin" is a heartfelt tribute written by Benjamin Franklin in memory of his brother, John Franklin, who passed away in 1756.

Presented here in its entirety, this letter reflects Benjamin Franklin's deep affection for his brother and offers words of comfort and encouragement to his sister-in-law during a difficult time of loss.

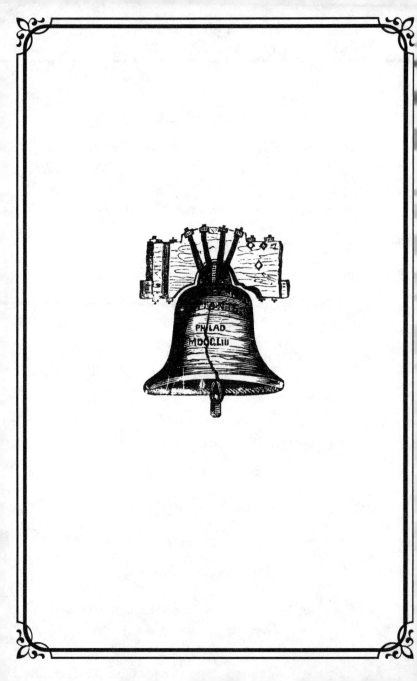

KEY EVENTS &
ACHIEVEMENTS

A Timeline of Benjamin Franklin's Life and Its Impact

Here is a timeline highlighting some of the most important moments in Benjamin Franklin's life and beyond.

1706: Benjamin Franklin is born in Boston, Massachusetts on January 17.

1723: Franklin runs away from his apprenticeship and moves to Philadelphia.

1729: Franklin opens his own printing shop in Philadelphia.

1732: Franklin begins publishing *Poor Richard's Almanack*.

1736: Franklin creates the Union Fire Company, the first fire department in Philadelphia.

1748: Franklin invents the Franklin stove, improving heating efficiency.

1752: Franklin conducts his famous kite experiment, demonstrating the electrical nature of lightning.

1754: Franklin proposes the Albany Plan of Union, a precursor to the United States Constitution.

1757: Franklin travels to England as a colonial representative for Pennsylvania.

1758: Franklin is appointed as the colonial agent for Pennsylvania in London.

1760: Franklin invents the glass armonica, a musical instrument.

1766: Franklin testifies before the British House of Commons in opposition to the Stamp Act.

1775: Franklin is appointed as a delegate to the Second Continental Congress.

1776: Franklin helps draft the Declaration of Independence.

1777: Franklin secures a critical military alliance with France during the American Revolutionary War.

1783: Franklin negotiates the Treaty of Paris, ending the Revolutionary War.

1785: Franklin serves as the United States' ambassador to France.

1787: Franklin is the oldest delegate at the Constitutional Convention in Philadelphia.

1789: Franklin becomes the president of the Pennsylvania Society for Promoting the Abolition of Slavery.

1790: Franklin dies on April 17 in Philadelphia at the age of 84.

1791: Franklin's autobiography, *The Autobiography of Benjamin Franklin,* is published posthumously.

1793: The University of Pennsylvania opens, with Franklin as its founder.

1806: Franklin's last will and testament establishes the Benjamin Franklin Trust.

1847: A monument to Franklin is erected in Philadelphia's Franklin Square.

1856: Franklin is inducted into the Hall of Fame for Great Americans.

1867: The Franklin Institute, a science museum and educational center, is founded in Philadelphia.

1926: The United States Postal Service issues the first postage stamp featuring Franklin.

1940: Franklin is featured on the $100 bill, which is still in circulation today.

REFERENCES

To learn more about this book, including access to a detailed list of resources for the quotes referenced in this work, please visit travishellstrom.com/franklin.